AUTHOR. A.SADAM HUSAIN HASANI
PERSONALITY DEVELOPMENT GUIDE
BE A FULFILLED
PERSON
BE A FULFILLED PERSON
BE A FULFILLED PERSON

Preface

Are you a fulfilled person?

This is the first question that every human being born in this world should ask himself. On the contrary if you ask me "Who is that fulfilled person.? Then remember well this book which i have written is only for you...!

Don't think that when I say fulfilled man here, I am going to talk about some man who has received all his body parts in order in his mother's womb. On the contrary, in this book I am going to explain when a man makes his life fulfilled and how he can achieve it. Of course, I step into the book with the support that this little book of mine will be of great help in developing you into a better personality and further fulfilling your life.

We must first clearly understand who the fulfilled person is. I think it would be best to explain here who the fulfilled person is. So first of all let's find out who that fulfilled person is.

Who is the fulfilled person?

First of all, I wish to present before you the real fact that only if one attains these three fundamentals which I mention below, the world can consider him as a fulfilled person.

Those three fundamentals.

1.Healthy

2.Wealthy

3.Characters

Even if a man has lost one of these three, the world is never ready to consider him as a fulfilled person. Because the world is very sure that the fulfillment of a man can only be achieved by these three fundamentals together. That is what I am also believing. Because you are very healthy but if you don't have wealth, is the world ready to accept you as a fulfilled person..? Please ask yourself for a moment. You will definitely get "No" instead..!

So every child born in the world must have these three fundamentals together to become the fulfilled person that this world is looking for. No matter whose child that child should be born with these three fundamentals to fulfill himself. Even if our minds refuse to accept this bitter truth and none of us can be exceptions, So we have to adapt to them due to the compulsion of time.

If you have got all these three fundamentals together, close your eyes for a moment and thank your Lord, because you are truly blessed in this world. So, once again I request you to keep in your attention that the fulfillment of a person is obtained from these three fundamentals together and next, I step into the first part of this book to analyze how much health is essential for the fulfillment of a person.?

Chapter 1

1.Health makes a man fulfilled person

We can see in history that many religions in this world and it's leaders have taught that health is the best fundamental for every human being in the world.

Yes Gandhi ji: He has said that health is the only real wealth in this world than gold and silver. In the same way, we can see in history that the Prophet Muhammad taught his people: "The first wealth that people should ask God for in this world is health. "In this way we can see that the Buddha also taught that "physical health is the greatest wealth in the world."

We can also see that all those sages who realized the superiority of physical health have established themselves in this world as "Fulfilled persons". In fact we can include two types of human beings in this world. One is a person who is sick and struggling to regain his health and another is who is struggling to maintain his health. Consider for a moment which of these two characters you are.? So keep in mind that health is the basic aspect that man should always maintain in his life.

Considering that many of us know a few things about the necessity of health, but we are not aware of its clear meaning, So I would like to point out its clear meaning first of all. Because I believe that it will be very helpful in creating a greater understanding of health. So let's see it..!

What is health?

"Health is when we are free to act as we wish."
Yes, that time when we are physically free is the springtime available in our life. Every human being in the world craves this time of freedom. It is a personal greed buried within every human being to do whatever they want freely without any restrictions. To most people it passes off as mere green. Although I have mentioned some methods of maintaining health in this book, there is one more thing I want from you that ""You must realize how important your physical health is to you."

"Yes"
Please don't get into the situation where someone is always advising you how to protect your health. In fact I think there is nothing more unfortunate for a man than that. So make maintaining your physical health only the first goal of your life. Because never forget that when you become unhealthy, you not only lose your freedom but also the freedom of those around you.

We can take the blind as a perfect example of this. They always become needy towards another human being. And yet they become empty corpses, left alone and wretched to not admire this wonderful world, and totter in the dark world. So I believe that this small example is enough because the condition of those blind people explains the true meaning and necessity of health very clearly. Next, I think it will be very useful to share some methods with you on how to maintain health, which is the basic requirement of this human society, so let's see some details about that too..!

How to maintain health.?

Here I am mentioning four important steps that we must follow at all times to maintain health.
Those are:
1.Having Food
2.Having Rest
3.Doing Exercise
4.Being Cleanliness

Now let's look at each of the above four methods in detail regarding how to follow them properly.

1. Dietary habits

The first factor to protect our health is our dietary habits. So let's see a few things about them here. First of all, we can divide food habits into two parts here.

1. The food we choose for ourselves.

2.The food we should avoid for ourselves.
So let's see what kind of food we can choose for ourselves

What foods to be chosen?

In today's era, we are forced to check multiple times at all times whether the food we choose for ourselves is fit for us to eat. If you ask that.! How to test it? Here I mention two general rules for that.

1.It should be clean.

2.It should be delicious.

I consider the first secret trick to maintaining our health is to always avoid foods beyond these two rules.

Yes..! Never forget that unclean food is the first enemy of your health. Many doctors point out that unhygienic food is the main cause of diseases like diarrhea and vomiting. Similarly, doctors warn us that viral fevers like cholera and typhoid are also spread by the snacks sold in open spaces on the side of the streets. So choose as many healthy foods as you can.

Next, there is nothing wrong with focusing on choosing delicious food for ourselves. Many of us are ready to pay a lot of money for expensive food items, but many times we fail to notice that that's taste like our traditional food. Just for the name of foreign food, we forget its taste and effect and eat it at a high price. They are very salty and taste unpleasant to us, but we swallow them with our teeth. Contrary to these, I fully believe that the best way to maintain our health is to cook and eat our traditional food very deliciously.

One more thing I am bound to point out here is that many of us think that if we want to preserve our health, we must eat half cooked tasteless food. But the truth is that even half cooked food is considered high in nutrients
Many doctors point out that when they are properly and thoroughly cooked, full power is also available. So it is my humble request that you enjoy clean and delicious food to your heart's content and I humbly ask you to never forget that you are solely responsible for your health while eating like this.

2. What foods should be avoided?

All kinds of food that looks ugly and dirty are foods that we should never eat. It is best for a person who wants to fulfill himself to completely avoid any of them, especially intoxicating foods. Because always remember that drugs like alcohol are the worst enemy of the human body that consumes health. Build a wall around you so they don't take place in any situation of your life. I can definitely promise that your health will definitely long last.

Similarly, I think it is better to avoid the meat of unclean animals as much as possible although they are cooked in the highest flavor. So it is my personal opinion that it is good to have specific restrictions on most of us because of indigestion and obesity. Likewise, I say that we often avoid eating meat. So many people question whether it is sinful to eat meat.? So it is very useful for all of us to give a few explanations about meat eating so let's see it too.

Eating meat is sinful ..?

Today, billions of people in the world are hungry and starving even for a meal. But On the other hand, I think the curse of this human society is that the huge cultural war is going on of whose food culture is the best.?

Once upon a time the man ate for life and health but now he is forced to keep his eating, religious and cultural pride.I think it is the horror of this era. Because Today's people eat some food only for the culture of society even if they don't like it totally, and some of those don't eat some healthy food for the culture of society even if they like it more.

I notice that many people here are deceiving themselves, wondering about their cultural pride. It's really awful. So I think it is very good to describe some things here in detail, how the cultural or religious -based food created and how we choose an independent healthy diet system. So come on, let's look at a few explanations ..!

How did food culture appear?

I am particularly concerned with meat, So I am writing more about them here. We can see in history that meat has played an important part in human food culture from the Stone Age to this time. And we can see areas from that time to the present where people could not survive unless they ate meat such as fish or meat. It is also worth noting the fact that grain and vegetables are not grown that is the main factor for meat being the exclusive food there. In some countries like India, we can see in history that the majority of the people living in the region have been eating both because grain, vegetable and meat are available in almost equal condition.

Especially within India we can see that the food habits were different according to the regions. For example, those in the southern part of the country had a high yield of rice, so they made rice their only staple food. Similarly we can understand through history that the people in the north have made wheat their special food because the yield of wheat was high in their area. It is also noteworthy here that in some parts of the Asian continent, grains such as millet and pulses are considered special foods.

So, I would like to emphasize here that first of all we should understand that the food habits of the people are based on the state of the land and according to each part of the region, and there is no reason to say that it is a religion-based food or a culture-based food. So it is enough if we deeply realize that the food culture was considered by the region and still looking by the condition of the soil there then I think we can solve most of today's diet-related cultural problems and controversies.

Next, as there are various confusions among people about which diet is best, So I am going to record some related explanations here.

What kind of diet can we choose?

Although there are many different foods in different tastes in the world today, the basic rules for them are two, as I mentioned above.

1. It should be in our favorite flavor.

2.2. It should be pure food that does not harm health.

My personal opinion is that any food that contains these two general rules can be eaten. Meat lovers can eat them liberally if they feel that it will not affect their health. Similarly those who like only vegetable food can eat them liberally if they feel that it will not affect their health. Among these, I think it is a very disgraceful act to insist that others should not like what you do not like or that everyone should like what you like by claiming it is food culture and food tradition.

So choosing meat and vegetables according to one's taste and according to one's physical condition is the best diet and I really think that is the height of indecency to try to impose one's eating habits on another in the name of religion or culture.

Some people ask that meat is often seen as unclean, so can all meat be eaten? So I would like to record some explanations here about it also.

Can we eat all meat?

I have mentioned in various places that the first rule for a man to take something as his food in this world is that it should be clean.So my opinion is that whether it is meat, or whether it is vegetable, eat it only if it is clean.I always insist on avoiding the meats of animals that eat only filth and are ugly to look at.I think it is best to avoid such meats just as we avoid poisonous plants.So if you ask can we eat all meat,? My point of view is that it is better to avoid meat that is still in an unclean state, which is harmful to one's health.

Finally, when we talk about meat, the first thing that comes to mind for many people in India is beef. So let's look at some things related to that here.

Can we eat beef..?

First of all I would like to remind you here that the cow is actually a great animal that contributes to this human society in many ways. In fact, I think it is not an exaggeration to say that it is a lovable pet that has become a part of the lives of farmers. Because they love such an animal beyond measure, they sanctify it as God. The problem arises from insisting that everyone else should see them in their way, even if we take it as their personal preference.

Because, as they think, a goat lover loves his goat too much and starts saying that no one should eat it anymore. Similarly, if everyone starts insisting not to eat a certain food by citing the sanctity of every object in the world, then the human being will not be able to eat anything in the world.

So I fervently request that those who love cows and hate eating beef please understand that it is best to refrain from doing it and to force others to do so is the height of indecency.In the same way, I am pointing out here that if certain people consider cow as sacred, avoiding beef before them will be a good practice for those who eat it.

So If you ask me, can we eat beef? I would like to say that it is their choice to eat or not to eat them, but if we feel that eating them hurts someone's mind, then I think it is better to avoid it.
So I believe that if we set up our food system as mentioned above to protect our health, we can protect ourselves to some extent. Try it if you like...!

Next, let's take a look at rest. Because It is very important for us to protect our health.

2.Rest related habits

Here we can see two types of rest:

1.Physical relaxation

2.Mental relaxation.

How to get rest physically?

We can take two types of physical relaxation.

1.Rest of Sleep

2.Rest of Interval

When we look at physical rest, the first place among them is sleep only, so let's look at some explanations related to it.

Various medical studies indicate that sleep is the only way in this world that we can keep our body refreshed and restored again and again. Similarly, many doctors point out that most of the people who do not sleep regularly are affected by serious diseases. They also point out that lack of sleep is the root of all diseases.

So if you desire to preserve your health please devote your rest periods to relaxing the body. Otherwise, do not lose your physical health by doing physical labor or engaging in some other entertainment even in your spare time. Because sleep is a great activity in our life. We should always maintain it. Here I am mentioning some of the benefits of sleep. I am sure it will be useful for you.

Sleeping is a noble act.

Many who run to conquer this world think that sleep is an unnecessary thing that puts our body in a state of inactivity. Similarly, they are not even ready to accept that sleep is a necessary human activity. Even they assumed that man is forced to do it as a daily ritual without any other means. But the truth is I believe that the most noble function of human activity is sleep.

Yes..!

It is very necessary to keep his body and movements in a state of inactivity as he is active with his body and movements at most time. It is not some ritual or ritual performed by man, rather it is the life recovery of every human being. This is what spiritual masters refer to as sleep as a small death. It is said that man survives every day through sleep. Scientific researchers are also realizing this. It means that after a man wakes up, he passes the past with his body and thoughts and therefore he often appears in this world as a new man everyday.

Therefore, I request here that each of us should understand that sleep is a wonderful movement or noble act in our lives, and it is not an empty ritual that makes our life inactive.

Next, let's look at some of the important health benefits that a person gets from sleeping.

Benefits of sleep.

1.It gives more energy and freshness to the brain.

In general, the brain of the human body is mostly active.But when man sleeps, the brain ceases its external activities and begins the work of retrieving all that it had previously recorded, recording only the most influential of them in the internal register, and throwing out the unnecessary things.Scientists point out that with this a person can recognize in a second something that he felt 50 years ago.It is also pointed out that sleep is the cause of such enormous capacity.

2. It Makes the heart beat regularly.

The heart beats in various ways when man is active outside and when he sleeps it defends himself from their effects and returns him to normal state. Many of the doctors explain that sleep mostly improves our blood circulation and protects us from heart diseases. In the same way, the heart immediately cleans the blood it receives and sends it out, but it is also said that the heart can do the work of cleaning the blood very smoothly, especially during sleep.

3. It Increases power of focus

Psychologists point out that all the old scenes and incidents go to the subconscious through sleep, when a person wakes up with a good sleep, his focus and thinking power are working very fresh.So students are also advised to study after waking up.They explain that reading or learning is based on focus, it can be fully absorbed by a person who wakes up mostly from the good sleep.

4. It Increases immunity.

Most doctors mention that when a person sleeps well, his body produces a lot of immune cells.For this reason that sleep is sometimes prescribed as a medicine for those who are ill.

5. Refreshes the body.

Man naturally faces laziness at a certain point of time as his body works a lot while he is awake.Doctors say that at such times man cannot get any better relief than sleep.Therefore, it is certainly not an exaggeration if sleep is the greatest gift given to man by God to relieve his physical laziness and refresh himself again and again.

So the benefits of sleep apart from the above are many more but I fear that by pointing them all out here I will bore your reading.So I am humbly asking you to stop thinking that sleep is just a small ritual in our life and please realize deeply that different parts of our lives are flourishing because of it.

Next, I would like to point out some explanations about what kind of effects we will face due to not sleeping properly..!

What are the effects of not sleeping properly?

1. It Causes heart disease.

Doctors strongly state that most heart diseases are caused by severe lack of sleep. Especially those who do not sleep properly are bound to suffer from high blood pressure or diabetes.

2.It Increases or decreases obesity.

Most doctors warn that lack of sleep can make us gain weight very fast and for some people it can make the body very leen.

3. It Causes skin diseases.

Doctors warn that lack of sleep is the closest cause of skin related diseases in the body.

4.It causes laxity in the brain.

Due to severe sleep deprivation, brain functions become completely impaired and become sluggish. Due to this, many of the doctors warn that the human's ability to think and his ability to pay attention is pushed to the worst level and in many cases this is the cause of mental retardation. So it is very possible for a person to get various problems affecting physical health due to lack of proper sleep.
Apart from these, researchers have also explained what happens when a person does not sleep at all. They state that on average a human being can live from 3 or 4 days to 11 days without sleep and beyond that a human being will at most die or completely lose his physical function. So don't ever imagine complete lack of sleep in your life.
I see this problem especially with night workers. They work at night and remain sleepless during the day. I kindly ask you to remember that this is a dangerous act that puts your body in huge danger.

Well, so far we have seen some explanations about the effects of not sleeping properly, now let's see some explanations about the effects of sleeping too much on our health.

Can we sleep more?

Before we look at oversleeping, it is important to know what oversleeping is. Similarly, it would be more appropriate to know how many hours a person sleeps on an average and how good his health is. So let's first find out how many hours an average human should sleep.

What is the average sleep time of a human being?

3 to 5 years old   = 10 to 13 hours.

6 to 12 years old   = 9 to 12 hours.

13 to 18 years old   = 8 to 10 hours.

19 to 60 years old   = 7 to 8 hours.

Doctors say that if a person of any age is sick then he can sleep for 14 to 18 hours based on medicine.Similarly,they indicate that for (baby)newborns also 16 to 18 hours of sleep is healthy.So I think you have some understanding of who should sleep for how long on average.So let's look at some explanations about sleep more.

Can we sleep more?

Doctors warn that sleeping beyond the above mentioned time will definitely affect the health. In particular, they warn those who are between the ages of 19 and 60 if they sleep more than 14 hours continuously, they will have hypersomnia. So they are always seen in a state of sleepiness. They also warn that it is the most deadly disease that can infect a human being. So always keep in mind that most doctors describe too much sleep as one of the biggest health risks.

Next some people ask that we try to sleep at a certain time but sleep does not come at the average hour you specified. So below I am recording some methods for average sleep. If possible, follow them too. I am sure you will get good results.

Methods of average sleep.

1. Choose a specific time to go to bed every day.

2. Make the bedroom moderately cool for sleeping.

3.Keep the bedroom mostly moderately dark.

4.Do not keep anything in the room that disturbs sleep.

5.Choose thin clothes mostly for sleeping.

6.Choose a soft bed.

7.Relax your body with a quiet prayer or reading a book before going to bed.

8.Sleep as much as possible in a place where the morning sunlight hits your body.

If you try to sleep as above I believe you will be able to get average sleep.

2.Short break as an interval.

Don't think that physical rest is only about sleeping. Instead, the best way to rest is to sit quietly and relax your body for a while you continue to work. This method is called Interval in all fields today. Because naturally, when the human body continues to be engaged in something for a long time, the activity begins to slip and decrease. Thus, the body becomes tired and unmotivated. In order to repair this, we are forced to take some rest from time to time. So never forget that such a little rest is very helpful to protect and empower our health.

Next, I will briefly describe here how much mental rest is necessary for us.

2.Mental relaxation.

I would like to mention here that mental rest is to calm the mind and improve the flow of thoughts. This mental rest is very helpful in improving our flow of thoughts and keeping us always fresh. Similarly, it is also true that people who are deprived of this peace of mind cannot live a healthy life. I think that all religions and its leaders have taught us the method of worship to get such peace of mind. So my view is that there is nothing wrong with setting aside a few minutes each day to strengthen your state of mind and clear your thoughts, which can greatly improve your health. I believe that doing this will help you to calm your mind and make better decisions and keep you fresh all the time.

To get this kind of relaxation you can do your religious meditations at some point, or go to a quiet place for a while, or listen to soft music or soothing songs. It is my belief that your mental and physical health can be protected by these.

Next, I feel obliged to mention how important exercise is to protect our health, so let's take a closer look at that too..!

3.Doing exercise.

Although exercise is not as necessary to maintain physical health as food and rest are, I believe that exercise is an essential requirement for maintaining our physical health. Exercising makes our body stronger, but it is an undeniable fact that our mind also gets stronger. According to philosophy, exercise is a great remedy for removing the old garbage that stays in our minds and thoughts.

In fact, when we start exercising for our health, we start loving ourselves. It is a fact that when we start loving ourselves, our body starts looking fresher.

So dear friends.!

Make sure to set aside 30 minutes of your 24 hours each day for exercise as much as you can. Take a closer look at your mental state after this 30minute workout and I can assure you that it will definitely look very refreshing. Perhaps if you find exercise too difficult, you can choose sports of your choice, such as tennis or volleyball, which can refresh the body. If you don't like to do that, you can definitely keep your body healthy by pedaling the bicycle for a long distance. If you don't want to do that, you can maintain your physical strength by practicing karate, stick swing, swimming, knife throwing etc.

So it is my kind request that you choose your exercise in any of the above ways. Because it is my deep belief that any one of these can keep your body healthy. Next, cleanliness is the foundation of our health, so let's take a closer look at them.

4.Being cleanliness

Before I explain to you how important cleanliness is, here I will tell you what is cleanliness.? I think it is best to explain.

What is cleanliness?

In today's general view, anything that does not harm other living things and which is attractive to look at is considered clean. Based on this we can say that all things having both the above characteristics are cleanliness.SO I think the correct meaning for cleanliness is "harmless and attractiveness".

We can see that all religions teach us to observe such cleanliness and such cleanliness is a great shield to protect us from disease. Because all the doctors agree that diseases develop from wherever there is pollution. They also point out that mosquitoes that spread diseases especially originate from polluted places.

So dear friends.!

First of all I emphasize here that the place where we are should be very clean. Even if your house is a cottage, keep it cleanly decorated and attractive to look at.

Next, to maintain physical cleanliness, remove nails, remove unwanted hair, wash the whole body with water, and clean the teeth and mouth from time to time. I believe that if we follow these all the time, we can definitely protect our health.

Similarly, it is best to wash our clothes in good water and dry them in the light of sun to get the cleanliness of clothes. If you can get over them and wear them after rubbing the iron box, they can look very clean and attractive.

Psychologists also point out that if we are very clean, our mental stability and mental happiness increases. It creates goodwill for those around you. We should never fail to note that being truly clean not only benefits us but also benefits those around us. I am obliged to remind here that today's real world is giving us evidence which society has made cleanliness its star mantra that society has become a prosperous society. Based on this we can see that all religions and it's leaders have left teaching cleanliness as the main duty.

The Prophet Mohammed said:
that "Cleanliness is the sign of God's faith".
In the same way, it can be seen that he mentioned that before every prayer one should worship God while purifying himself, which emphasizes what is necessary for a clean person.

So dear friends.!

Always maintain cleanliness.!

By asking you to protect your precious health as a treasure, I step into the second part of this book by reminding you once again that the main objective of this first part is a healthy life that makes us a fulfilled person.

Chapter 2

Wealth only makes a man fulfilled.

For a man to be seen as a fulfilled person in this world, it is as necessary for him to be healthy as it is for him to be rich and prosperous. It is a fact that any man who is not rich in this world he is not seen by the people as a fulfilled man. Many of us may have different views about money and wealth, but in this book I would like to explain in depth how money is essential to human life and what kind of bond it has with us and those around us.

But it is very important for us to know that, what is prosperity? So I will record a small explanation about them here.

What is prosperity?

Amassing a large amount of "money" and "valuable assets" is called wealth or prosperity. Apart from these, many economists point out that the things we have for our needs cannot be called Wealthy. So we can refer to those who have a large amount of material or wealth as wealthy.

Well, those who have a lot of wealth should be left as wealth merchants. But I think your next question will be whether there is any way to become such a wealthy merchant.?

Be a little patient, for that now I am going to mention two ways. Read carefully. I believe that if you do these two things well, it will be enough for you to become a rich merchant.

1. You must understand the value of money.

2.Learn to earn income in multiple ways.

My point of view is that those who do not execute these two ways properly cannot become wealthy merchant. So I will explain briefly here on the basis that it will be more beneficial for everyone to give a little explanation about both of them.

1.1. Value of money.

It is true that many of us think that love, affection and relationships are better than anything else in this world, but no one here can deny that money is the foundation to build all of them.I see many people who say that they have no desire for money as fakes. In reality, they are very greedy.

It is true that money does not bring happiness, but it is even more true that without it we lose our peace.Because prosperity is higher than poverty. Uncomfortable poverty is never equal to wealth freedom.

Do you think there is anything greater happiness in this world than his wages for a really hard working employee.? In fact, behind every drop of his sweat, his family's happiness is a secret known only to him. I can't say that money is everything but I can't deny that various things are done here only because of money. You may indeed be non-worldly, but don't forget that you too have to live in this money-driven world.

Yes my dear friends..!

Never forget that money makes many of the rules in the game of life. I can't say that we should cry for it. Because money will never cry for us. I think there is nothing wrong with having money in your pocket. But it is my humble opinion that letting it dominate our mind is the biggest danger.

So realize the value of money.
Otherwise, give up the idea of becoming rich. Next, I have mentioned above that if you want to be a rich merchant, you should be able to earn income in many ways. Let's see some things related to it here.!.

2.Generating income in multiple ways.

The best way for us to become super rich is to understand the business that generates income in multiple ways. Many of us think that we can get great wealth only by cheating. And yet they console themselves by saying that they are poor so far because they have not cheated anyone yet. I think this is a manifestation of their incompetence and ignorance.
Because it is the basic rule of business strategy that you can reach the greatest heights in business only if you are honest. I would also like to point out here that we should never forget that many of the flag bearers in business today are honest workers.

Similarly, some of us shy away from the pursuit of great wealth, thinking that one must be full of knowledge and skill to attain great wealth. Although it is true that knowledge and skills are required to succeed in business, we cannot deny that it is 100% true that all of us can develop them.

So, most of the thoughts of those who cannot accumulate great wealth today are the same as I mentioned above. It is also a fact that those thoughts are the main reason for their being poor.

So my dear friends..!

If you want to become wealthy, you must be ready to jump into multiple income generating businesses. You should also have the willpower to invest in such a business. Only if you are ready to invest in a small or big business, you can take the next step towards wealth prosperity.

My humble request is that if you are not ready to invest and trade then please put aside your dream of becoming rich and prosperous.

Many of us earned hard but forgot to learn the art of doubling it. Many times we focus on keeping it locked and protected. This is what I see as the characteristic of the poor. But wealthy people don't do that. Instead, they are willing to boldly invest the rest in other businesses, thereby increasing their income.

So my dear friends.! If you want to become rich and prosperous you should be ready to invest your wealth in various ways of income generating business. Keep it in your subconscious mind that this is the only way to double your wealth.

Now you may ask, we want to increase our income, but we don't know how to start it. Don't worry, here I will mention some best ways for them.

How to start a business?

When starting a business do not fail to consider these three rules that I mention below.

1. Even if you don't have complete knowledge about the business you are about to start, don't fail to check yourself several times if you have the ability to handle them. Because many of us hope to invest in some business and increase our income. So we trust some people and start a business, but in some situations when that person leaves it, we are unable to deal with it and we lose our investment completely. So always avoid trusting others to invest in business that you cannot handle as much as possible. This way you can protect your economy.

2. Do not fail to evaluate how necessary the business you are about to start is for the people in your area. Because many of us have the desire to do business, but we fail to know how necessary the product is for the people in the area.?
For example, if you pour your entire investment into a product that people have no need for, it is equivalent to pouring your entire wealth into the ocean. So if you want to grow your wealth safely, learn to know people's needs first.

3. Even if you have a lot of wealth, start with a small investment when you first start your business. Because many of us, when we first start a business, invest our entire wealth in a huge way. But when it fails, we fail to save enough money to deal with it, and our entire investment is crippled in it and we are forced into huge difficulty. So never forget to save some money for difficult situations in business. So before you start a business, never fail to take these three into consideration. I believe that these three rules will surely protect your business. Also, I think it will be very useful for everyone to write here about how to double the business you have started. So let's look at some things here.

How to double your business?

Business is based on two rules.

1.Quality Products.
2.Customers.(Marketing)

Let's look at a few things related to quality products.

1.Quality Products.

If you want your business to thrive, the first thing you should focus on is the quality of your product. Because never forget that people want to get value for their money first, so it is your prime duty to check the quality of your product from time to time. Next, set the right price for the product, because people care about the price of the product as much as they care about its quality. So I believe that the best way to grow your business is to determine your profit based on people's satisfaction as much as possible.

Next, let's look at a few things related to Customer or marketing.

2.Customer & Marketing

No matter how good your product is, you need to know how to market it to people's expectations. Many people think of marketing as hard work. In reality, marketing is all about getting customers to buy your product with satisfaction over and over again. Simply you need to turn your customer into a regular customer, because never forget that your income is entirely dependent on the flow of your customers. So below I will mention some ways to attract your customers.

Ways to attract customers.

1. You should always greet customers with a smile.
2. Let the customer's needs be told first by their mouths. Then you should kindly introduce the products you have.
3. Avoid arguing with customers altogether.
4.Small discounts should be announced from time to time.
5.You should have some technique in place so that your customers can contact you directly, whether by your phone number, or through the internet.
6.You should also invite good customers for some of your home celebrations.
7.Try to make as many big customers as possible into business friends.

I believe that if you follow some of the above strategies in your business, your business will surely prosper. So implement it as much as you can.

Next, the biggest problem faced by most of the traders is the loss in the business. How to deal with such loss is also a little detailed here, as it will be useful for everyone, I am recording them here as well.

How to protect the business without loss?

1. Be prepared to face competition and loss.

First of all, you need to understand that there are many chances of loss or competition in your business, and my first request is to develop the mental strength to deal with them all. Because most entrepreneurs close their business and run away after seeing a small loss. They do not even come forward to see why their business has suffered losses.
Next, many of us do not like competition in business. If another person does business against us, we immediately start looking at him with hatred. But economists point out that business is competition. And they say that we must understand that it is natural for us to trade for whatever wealth we seek that will be sought by another also.

Therefore, they advise that we should meet business competition in a beautiful manner and beyond them, we should use our competitors as our business assistants. So when you jump into trading, first you need to develop the mental strength to face competition and losses.

2. Must keep track of budgets.

I know the main reason most people lose money in business is because they don't keep track of their business expenses. So if you start a business first keep a software or a ledger to keep track of them. Keep recording everything from the investment amount to the accounts of the day. Especially the expenses spent on the purchase of the business, the expenses incurred to maintain the business, and the salary expenses spent on the workers. Try to find out your profit once a month as much as possible.

3.Buy more of what's on sale.

In your business, you need to know which items are selling the most and which items are selling the least. Buy and stock the best selling items in your business so you can grow your business without saying no to people. In the same way, avoid buying and hoarding any item that is not selling properly, because we can see that most people are very disappointed in this matter and are facing huge losses. Because keep in mind that unsold goods become a burden rather than a profit for us.

If perhaps your business is running at a heavy loss then try to follow some of the steps I mention below.

How to deal with loss.?

There are only two ways to deal with losses in our business.

1.You have to be prepared to continue the business for a while with no profit.

2. You should innovate your business and offer some discounts to suit the
people.
I am obliged to remind you that these can only cover your losses in two ways.

Next, if you invest only your labor without investing, then let's see a few things
about how to create wealth and prosperity.

Can you become rich without investing?

Above I mentioned that the basic rule of richness is to invest in a business to keep doubling your wealth. That business may be manufacturing and selling products, or buying and selling certain products in bulk. But on the complete opposite of them, my position is that if you can invest only your ability and increase your wealth, it will definitely be possible. Moreover, I can also mention that this is a risk free business. I mention a few such tasks below.

1. Being a Government servant.
2. Being a politician.
3.Being a teacher.
4. Being doctors.
5.Being a bank employee.
6. Being house and land brokers.
7. Being interpreters.
8. Being communicators.
9.Being a repairer of goods.

There is no doubt that your wealth will surely continue in all these, but here I will only remind you that you should know how to save the income that comes and use it regularly.

Next I know the only question you are left with is how someone can become rich with no investment and no proper skills..!
I will shortly mention a few explanations for them considering the summary of the book..!

Learn, collect money, then jump in business.

First of all you have to understand that everyone in this world is not born learning everything and not born with everything. So learn to be a good worker to trade first. My warm request is to identify the pitfalls in the business and then start collecting a certain amount of money to start a business.

Next, it will be very useful to mention how to collect, so I will explain it here a little bit more.

How to collect money.?

1. First make sure why you are saving money for.?

2. Decide how much you need for your business.

3.Set aside one-tenth of your income for savings.

4.Don't buy anything just for luxury.

5.Choose and buy the product you need that will last for a long time and avoid the need for frequent repairs or renewal.

6.Do not buy goods sold in installments and accumulate them at home forever. I promise you that if you manage your money like this, you will surely become rich one day. Never forget that if you don't make any savings on your income, you're probably just watering in the bucket which has a big hole.

Finally, I would like to conclude this second part of this book by pointing out to you some reasons why a poor man remains poor and why a rich man remains rich.

The poor and the rich.

1.A rich person is always ready to learn new things. But a poor person is never ready to learn anything new.

2.A rich person is always moving towards a goal of his own, but a poor person is aimless.

3.A rich person will think more positively but a poor person will be negative no matter what.

4.A rich man is ready to take many hardships for progress, but a poor man turns his back and runs away when he sees hardships.

5.A rich person always spends more of his time in self-improvement, but a poor person spends more of his time in vain amusements.

6.A rich man is always looking for his own challenges, but a poor man is always looking for his own luckiness.

7.A rich person will always take responsibility for his own failure, but a poor person will try to make his failure as someone else's failure.

8.A rich man always considers the end results but a poor man tries to get away only considering his own incapacity.

9.A rich person will focus on investing and doubling his money, but a poor person will focus on spending more of his money.

10.A rich man sees his business as his passion, but a poor man keeps his business because others are doing it.

Take a moment to reflect on how you stand in the above. Instill in yourself the dream of becoming rich today.
Next let's go to the third part which is the main part of this book..!

Chapter 3

Good Character only makes as fulfilled person

The third part of this book is about good character, which I wished to set up in the first part. But this part needs to be explained in detail, that's why it needs to be set up in the third part. I am really sorry for that. I have chosen this section as the third one considering the book format but I fully believe that good character plays a major role in making a fulfilled man and really it plays the first role in personality.

Because I would say that if a man loses his wealth, it is not really a loss. Perhaps if a man loses his health, I take it that he has lost some important part of his life, but if a man loses his character, it is my firm belief that he has really lost a great part of his life.

Yes dear friends..!

Knowledge, power and wealth can bring us power, but only good character can bring us value. In the same way, beauty and talent can carry us to high places, but good character only has the power to sustain us. People may praise knowledge and power, but God only praises good characters, it has been said in the Vedas. It is an undeniable fact that many times a man's whole life is decided by his character.

Yes my dear Friends..!

Even if I mention that this good character is the reason for the success of the majority of winners, I think it is not an exaggeration, because good character is often powerful enough to surpass all abilities. And this world is ready to accept a good person as its leader, because this world believes that only a good person can bring many good developments in this world.

So my dear friends.!

My humble request is that if you want to become a fulfilled man then prepare to focus more on developing your good character or put away the dream of becoming a fulfilled man in this life and let your life go on its course without burdening anyone.

At last I again remind you that good character only plays a great role in fulfilling a man. Next we need to know what is good character so I am going to describe them briefly below.

What is a good character.?

"Psychologists refer to good character as seeking only the good without doing injustice to anyone."

They have divided these qualities into two categories.

Those are:

1. Characters we should develop in ourselves.

2.Characters we should avoid from ourselves.

Let us first see what are the characteristics that we need to develop in ourselves.

Characters to develop.

1. Honesty
2. Compassion
3. Caring
4. Humbleness
5. Forgiveness
6. Tolerance
7. Apologizing for mistakes.
8. Thanking
9. Simplicity
10. Being unique
11. Maintaining self-respect.

All the above mentioned characters are important characters that should be acquired in every human being. It is my humble request that every human being should strive in his life to develop these.

I think it will be very useful to explain here a little bit about how these wonderful characters are necessary for our life and how we can develop them. So let's take a look at them.

1.Honesty

I believe that honesty is the only great weapon that a man can strengthen himself in this world. It can also be mentioned that he does not need any laws or rules and regulations. Really I see an honest man as a miracle uniquely created by God.

Yes my dear friends..!

Never forget that in fact nothing will give you more respect than honesty.There is a strength in honesty. It is a fact that no one in the world can shake it. But it is a sad thing that most people do not realize it.

Let me also remind you that a study has shown that the happiest people in the world are actually honest people. Similarly, honesty may not get you many friends in many situations, but it is this honesty that brings you the right people. So be prepared to be honest if you want to be trusted. Give your honesty as a gift especially to those who love you. Because honesty is like water in relationships. It has no color, no shape, no taste, but it is the basic need of life, so never lose it.

Similarly Don't think that being too perfect is honest. Because no one can do it. But understand that honesty is being true to yourself and those who believe in yourself. And don't apologize to anyone for being honest, because honesty doesn't hurt any good, it hurts only lies.

I also point out here that trying to prove your honesty to others is the same as putting yourself in the act of diminishing yourself. So understand that it is only your responsibility to be honest not proven.

2.Compassion

Many of us think that showing compassion to others is a very difficult thing. But it is a fact that something more precious than that compassion cannot be given to anyone so easily. I think that kindness is the great beautiful thing in this world we show whether it is small or big.

Yes My dear friends..!

The only moment in your life that gives you the meaning of life is the moment you show compassion to others..! Because that's where you prove yourself as a real person. I think it is unfortunate that many of us forget that we are being lifted up by lifting others up. In fact, I believe that the sign that people live in this world is that they are compassionate.

So share small, big, kind words wherever you go. It can make a difference in someone's life. It can also be the factor that colors someone's dark life. In fact, show compassion even to unkind people, because they are the ones who need it the most. Don't get so wrapped up in your own well-being that you don't have time to think about others

Similarly, don't think that showing kindness is a weak act, because it takes a lot of courage to show kindness. Dear friends remember well..!

I believe that if anything has the power to change the world, it is compassion. So if you want to be loved by this world, plant your kindness wherever you go.. and wherever you go you will surely be loved.

3.Taking care.

In this fake world, there are many people who say and act they have a lot of love, but I see that there are very few people who actually practice it, because I believe that the sign of love is only caring.

Yes my dear friends..!

This care only strengthens the relationship between two people. The reason why many people's relationships break up is because of selfishness at the time of taking care. I think that there is no happier moment in a relationship than the care one person takes for another.

When I think of giving a structure to the care, I think a mother is only worthy of it. Because only mother is full of love. She does not hesitate to give it. In other words, I see her as a wonderful treasure who cares even in anger.

So my dear friends..!

Show your care as much as you can to those around you. Likewise, never lose those who care about you.

4.Humbleness

Humbleness is a sign of maturity. Wear it as your main garment. If you do that, no one can shake you. Because those who want to bring you down will either praise you to bring you down, or they will scold you to bring you down, but when you keep humble, you will not be affected by their actions. They will definitely lose. Humbleness is the beauty of a great man. He who has humbleness will go on to the heights. But whoever has the arrogance that "I am the best" he will fall into the same pit that he dug to bring people down.

So my dear friends..!

Please don't think that you are better than anyone else because everyone is unique in this world. Life teaches us humility from time to time, but we fail to learn from it. I think that when we start realizing that nothing in this world is permanent, we will definitely start practicing humbleness. In the same way, the clothes you wear in this world may be high, the house you stay in may be luxurious, but never forget that death and mud are the same for everyone.

So humbleness is the only challenge facing a successful person in this world. I think most people fail in this.

So my dear friends..!
Keep humble, own the heights..!

5.Forgiveness

Forgiveness is the greatest gift for the improvement of human relationships. It is a fact that any relationship without forgiveness will not last. They are the weak who take revenge because they do not have the willpower to forgive. But strong people forgive very easily and pass on because they know very well that there is no punishment in this world more severe than forgiveness. So don't think that forgiveness is weakness. Forgiveness takes a lot of strength.

Consider that your forgiveness can sometimes be an opportunity for someone to choose a better path in life. While forgiving someone does not change the wrong that was done, it can prevent it from happening again. Consider that your forgiveness can sometimes be an opportunity for someone to choose a better path in life. Forgiving someone does not change the wrong that was done, but it can prevent it from happening again.

Be sure to forgive each other in relationships. You are a mature person when you understand that everyone is human and that something goes wrong with everyone. Similerly learn to forgive yourself in the same way, because that is what has the power to get you out of the wrong you have done.

My dear friends..!

Forgiveness may seem like a simple thing to ask for, but it's only when you give it that you realize how much it's worth.

Forgive who surrounds you..! And Live happily..!

6.Tolerance

Patience is like the most delicious fruit that ripens in a long distance. You cannot get it very easily, but it is the fruit of your success.
Most of the people consider patience as a weakness but the truth is anger is the biggest weakness I know.

Yes.

He who has love and patience can build this world better. But he who does not have patience will cause even firmly built empires to crumble.
It is an undeniable fact that one minute of impatience can spoil 100 years of peace.

So my dear friends..!

Be patient. Understand that there is a time for everything. Deeply realize that nothing in this world can be built suddenly at the same time. Realize that the biggest test in your life is waiting for the opportunity you are looking for and your patience will surely reward that your great dream.

So believe that just because you don't get something today doesn't mean you won't get it tomorrow.

Be patient and make life meaningful.

7. Apologizing for mistakes.

Only forgiveness has the power to solve all the unsolvable problems in this world. If you make a mistake, ask for forgiveness without hesitation. That is the act of superiors. Many of us think that apologizing after a mistake lowers our self-esteem, but in reality, apologizing for our mistakes can actually increase our self-esteem. See take your apologize as an atonement for your actions Don't take it too seriously if the other person ignores it.

If your words hurt someone, immediately apologize for it.." Tell him instantly that it is not my intention to trouble you." I am so sorry"

My dear friends..!

Finally, if you want to say something to someone, please say, " I am Sorry..! As far as I know, that will be the last priceless thing you do in this world.

8.Thanking

Thanking someone for their help is a great trait. Because there are very few people who help in this world, we should take some time to thank those who have made good changes in our lives.I truly believe that there is no better prayer in this world for someone than to say thank you.
So don't hesitate to say thanks anywhere. Saying thanks is a noble act. It is proof of our goodness. It is also a wonderful trait that shows our humility.

If you don't show gratitude, it's like buying a nice gift and keeping it for yourself.

So say thank you..! Make the relationship last.

9.Simplicity

Simplicity is the sign of the wise person. Many people think that beauty belongs in luxury. But the truth is that simplicity gives more beauty. Luxury attracts the eyes, but simplicity attracts the mind. Beauty created by luxury always fails in front of simplicity. Therefore, as far as I know, the best dress worn by a high man in this world is simplicity.

Simplicity can be described in a single word as " that we choose what is necessary for us. Or " to be ourselves"

My dear friends..!

Understand that simplicity gives us more freedom.So learn to take only what is necessary for your life. Don't burden yourself with unnecessary luxury.

Nature and life are very easy, but realize that we are making it difficult.

So live simply ..Live freely ..!

10. Being unique

The only way to establish yourself in this world is to be unique. If you ask how to be unique?

'I would say you just be yourself .

Everyone in this world has a vision, a thought and an ability to act. Only those who execute it properly prove themselves uniquely in this world. It is also my belief that those who think that they can live their lives only by themselves can live uniquely in this world.

So color your life according to your thoughts on the white paper of your life. Don't make it a tissue to be used by others. Your life is not a shirt that someone else can wear on his measurement. It should be tailored according to your thoughts on your own measurement.

Don't compare yourself with others, it can only help to weaken your strength. Many people here are afraid to show themselves but my humble request is that you don't become one of them. Always keep developing yourself. There is a crowd in this world to follow you. Always be an example to others. Don't want to imitate anyone. Don't look for your approval from anyone. Be sure that there is no other person in this world who knows you better than you.

So Be unique..! and Establish yourself..!

11. Maintaining self-respect.

Never forget that when you respect yourself, others will respect you. It is up to you to decide how the world sees you. You have to decide how this world sees you. Keep in mind that your self-esteem determines your success. Never accept being disrespected. Openly ignore the place that disrespects you. Even if they call it arrogance.

Remember that no one can take away your self-respect without giving it a chance. Do not ask for respect from anyone, and do not allow anyone to disrespect you. Simply give your absence to those who don't respect your presence.

My Dear friends...!

Maintain self respect.
Protect your self-esteem.

I am also obliged to bring to your attention here how many benefits there are in this world due to your following of the above virtues.

The benefits of good characters.

1. Not harassing anyone.
2. Not insulting anyone.
3. Living in harmony.
4. To help.
5. Doing charity

 I will explain fully in the second part regarding these good deeds mentioned above, by God willing.

Now let's go to the final part of this book.
That is, let's take a closer look at what are the bad characteristics and its harm consequences in this world.

Bad characters

1. Cheap thought.
2. Arrogance.
3. Jealousy.
4. Greedy.
5. Angry.

Let's have a brief look at the above mentioned bad characters.

1. Cheap thought.

Cheap thought comes especially from cheap people. People who think about other people cheaply often behave cheap wherever they go.
People who have this mindset are like a broken wheel on a good vehicle. They can't move forward unless they remove that dirt. Although it is natural for all human beings to have evil thoughts, but good people get rid of it. Evil people also get caught in it.

Yes my dear friends..!

Never forget that your life is a reflection of your thoughts.
Your good thoughts are like the money you save in a bank, which you can use whenever you want for your benefit. But your bad thoughts are like the garbage you collect in a garbage bag, and as long as you have them, they will continue to stink.

So my dear friends.

Keep cleaning your mind from bad thoughts from time to time and try to keep your thoughts under your control. Otherwise it will keep you in its control and make your world a land of darkness.

And it will become a god that shows only the evil in this world to your eyes.

So avoid negative thoughts and celebrate your happy life...!

2. Arrogance.

Arrogance is a mental disease in the human mind. It is a kind of addiction to see that everyone is inferior and suppressed. People with this disease take pride in humiliating and insulting others. It is a fact that people do not like people with this kind of character and with this kind of people are often seen as ignorant.

In fact it is like a crow introducing itself as a peacock. They always spend their time speaking unnecessary pride or putting others down.

So my Dear friends..!

Be very careful with these kinds of people.
Mostly keep them far away, because you have to protect yourself from their disease.

3. Jealousy.

Jealousy is an expression of inferiority. Those who are jealous surely have inferiority. In other words, envious people are silly people who forget to think about their own abilities and think about others. They don't like other people's success. They try to be too focused on make down the actions of others, so they always seem unhappy.

It is also true that many times the envious people are the ones who make us feel our self-worth.
So My Dear friends..!
If someone is jealous of you, please don't hate them because they think you are superior to them.

As far as I know, jealousy is the weakest character in a human being. Don't ever choose it for yourself.
In fact, winners always make others their role models, but envious people often make others their enemies.

So my dear friends..!

Be a winner and don't lose your life by being jealous.

4. Greedy.

Greed is like a poison that entered into a great soul.
So those who are greedy do not know enough of this world.they can not feel by
anything happy.

This is what our great mahatma Gandhi said:

"This world is enough to satisfy everyone's needs, but not enough to satisfy the
greed of the greedy man,".

Yes, greed is like a big monster with a small mouth. No matter how much you
feed it, it is not enough for it. Due to this greed, many people are walking around
blindly unable to see various benefits in this world and are permanently addicted
to it.

So my dear friends..!

Realize that the greatest wealth you have is the absence of greed.then you can protect even your peace.

5. Angry.

Anger is not a wrong emotion. It is a necessary emotion. But I think each of us should learn how to use it.
First we need to understand why we should be angry. We should learn to be angry only with those who deserve our anger. Because I believe that if we understand that there are many ignorant people in this world, we will not be angry most of the time.

Always remember that we should not punish ourselves by our anger for someone else's stupidity. At most, if you get angry, stay calm. Because many of us think that we can do anything because we get angry, but in the end, it leads to great harm.

So my dear friends..!

You can be angry by thinking about what you don't like and you can be happy by thinking about what you like. Realize that your life depends on which of these two you choose. Control your anger. Enjoy your life full of happiness..!

It is my belief that if we avoid the above mentioned characters from ourselves we can make ourselves a fulfilled man. Try to avoid them as much as you can.

Next, I will point out below the consequences of having the above qualities on us and those around us.

Consequences of bad characters:

1. Injustice.
2. Killing, & Robbery.
3. Slander.
4. Cheating.
5. Gossip.
6. Make a bad identity.
7. Bad habits.

Let's see All this in more detail in Part II....!

Thank you :
Author.A.Sadam husain hasani

Blessing by:

As a mother I was very proud to see that my son A. Sadam Hussain Hasani
wrote this book day and night. I have read this book completely.
He has described very well how this human society can elevate itself and how an
individual can fulfill himself. I would like to convey my sincere wishes to give the
creations to this community. I pray forever that the almighty may accept his hard
work. I sincerely wish him to give such various useful opportunity for this society
by his journey of writing.

Your's:
Lovable Mother:A.Jarina Begum

NOTES

NOTES